# CAMBRIDGE PRIMARY
## Science

Learner's Book

**3**

Jon Board and Alan Cross

# CAMBRIDGE
## UNIVERSITY PRESS

University Printing House, Cambridge CB2 8BS, United Kingdom

Cambridge University Press is part of the University of Cambridge.

It furthers the University's mission by disseminating knowledge in the pursuit of education, learning and research at the highest international levels of excellence.

Information on this title: education.cambridge.org

© Cambridge University Press 2014

First published 2014
Reprinted 2015

Printed by Multivista Global Ltd, India

*A catalogue record for this publication is available from the British Library*

ISBN 978-1-107-61141-2 Paperback

Cambridge University Press has no responsibility for the persistence or accuracy of URLs for external or third-party internet websites referred to in this publication, and does not guarantee that any content on such websites is, or will remain, accurate or appropriate. Information regarding prices, travel timetables, and other factual information given in this work is correct at the time of first printing but Cambridge University Press does not guarantee the accuracy of such information thereafter.

Cover artwork: Bill Bolton

...................................................................................

# Introduction

The *Cambridge Primary Science* series has been developed to match the Cambridge International Examinations Primary Science curriculum framework. It is a fun, flexible and easy-to-use course that gives both learners and teachers the support they need. In keeping with the aims of the curriculum itself, it encourages learners to be actively engaged with the content, and to develop enquiry skills as well as subject knowledge.

This Learner's Book for Stage 3 covers all the content in Stage 3 of the curriculum framework. The topics are covered in the order in which they are presented in the curriculum for easy navigation, but can be taught in any order that is appropriate to you.

Throughout the book you will find ideas for practical activities, which will help learners to develop their scientific enquiry skills as well as introduce them to the thrill of scientific discovery.

The 'Talk about it!' question in each topic can be used as a starting point for classroom discussion, encouraging learners to use scientific vocabulary and develop their understanding.

'Check your progress' questions at the end of each unit can be used to assess learners' understanding. Learners who will be taking the Cambridge Primary Progression test for Stage 3 will find these questions useful preparation.

We strongly advise you to use the Teacher's Resource for Stage 3, ISBN 978-1-107-61150-4, alongside this book. This resource contains extensive guidance on all the topics, ideas for classroom activities, and guidance notes on all the activities presented in this Learner's Book. You will also find a large collection of worksheets, and answers to all the questions from the Stage 3 products.

Also available is the Activity Book for Stage 3, ISBN 978-1-107-61150-4. This book offers a variety of exercises to help learners consolidate understanding, practise vocabulary, apply knowledge to new situations and develop enquiry skills. Learners can complete the exercises in class or be given them as homework.

We hope you enjoy using this series.

With best wishes,
the Cambridge Primary Science team.

# Contents

# 1 Looking after plants

## 1.1 Plants and their parts

Plants can look very different.
Most have four main parts.

leaves – make food for the plant

flowers – help the plant to make seeds

stem – to transport water around the plant

roots – support the plant and collect water from the soil

## Activity 1.1

### Make a model plant

Make a plant like this one.

Make labels for the stem, roots, leaves and flower. Stick them to your plant.

**You will need:**
string • straws
coloured paper or card
sticky tape • glue

Healthy leaves.

Healthy plants have healthy roots, stems and leaves.

A plant with unhealthy roots, stems and leaves will not grow well.

Unhealthy roots with root knot disease.

Unhealthy leaves with rust disease.

A plant with healthy roots.

## Questions

1  List **four** things that most plants have.
2  Describe how plants are different from each other.

**Talk about it!**
Why don't plants have flowers all year round?

## *What you have learnt*

- Most plants have roots, a stem, leaves and flowers.
- Healthy plants have healthy roots, stem and leaves.
- A plant with unhealthy roots, stem and leaves will not grow well.

# 1.2 Plants need light and water

Sunil has an unhealthy plant.

What does a plant need to stay healthy and grow?

## Activity 1.2a

### Do plants need light to grow?

Look at the pictures to see what to do.

**You will need:**
six young plants • watering can • box to cover three plants

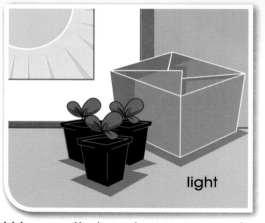

light

no light

Water all the plants every day.
What do you **predict** will happen to the leaves, stems and roots of the plants?
In this **investigation** both groups of plants are given water.
What else do you need to keep the same to make this a **fair test**?

If plants do not get enough light and water the roots, stem or leaves, become unhealthy. The plant will **wilt.**

Light and water both help the plant to make food.

## Activity 1.2b

### Do plants need water to grow?

Look at the pictures to see what to do.

Water every day.

Water twice a week.

Do not water.

What do you predict will happen to the plants' leaves, stems and roots in each case?

What do plants need to grow? How do you know?

**Explain** what you have found out.

The surface of the Moon.

## Questions

1 What does a plant need to grow and stay healthy?

2 Explain what happens to the stem and leaves when you put a plant in a dark place.

3 Would a plant grow if it was given juice instead of water? Draw a picture to show how you could investigate this.

**Talk about it!**

Could plants ever grow on the Moon?

## What you have learnt

- All plants need light to grow and keep their stems and leaves healthy.
- All plants need some water to grow and keep their stems and leaves healthy.

# 1.3 Transporting water

## The roots and the stem

Helene has a plant that looks unhealthy.
Look at the roots.

This pot is too small for the roots.

The roots are really close together and cannot absorb water well.

Putting the plant in a bigger pot will allow the roots to spread out.

The stem transports water to the leaves and flowers.

The roots absorb water from the soil.

The roots transport water to the stem.

## Activity 1.3

### Making plants go blue

**You will need:**
a white flower • some celery • a container of water
blue food colouring • a plastic knife

A plant stem can transport water to the leaves and flowers.
Predict what would happen if the water was blue.

**1** Your apparatus to use.
knife
dropper
white flower
food colouring
celery
container of water

**2** Place the celery and the flower in the water. Add a few drops of colouring.

After one day, cut the celery and look inside.
Can you explain what has happened to the celery and the flower?

## Questions

1 Why do plants sometimes need to be moved to a bigger pot?

2 How do plants get water to their leaves?

3 What would happen to a plant with no roots? Why?

**Talk about it!**
What happens to flowers when they are cut and put into water?

## What you have learnt

- Roots absorb water from the soil.
- Roots transport water to the stem.
- The stem transports water around the plant.

# 1.4 Plant growth and temperature

## Activity 1.4

**You will need:**
two similar bean plants • a thermometer • a ruler

**Words to learn**

thermometer    temperature

results    bar chart

conclusion

At which temperatures do plants grow best?

Set up an investigation like one of the pictures below.

Put one plant in the classroom.

Put one plant outside in cold weather.

Put one plant in the classroom.

Put one plant outside in warm weather.

Predict which plant will grow the best. Use a ruler to measure the height of the plants and a thermometer to measure the temperature every few days. Record your results in a table.

| Day | Cold/hot plant | | Warm plant | |
|-----|---------------|---|-----------|---|
| | Temperature in °C | Height in cm | Temperature in °C | Height in cm |
| 1 | | | | |

Draw a bar chart to show the height of the plants on the last day.
What is your conclusion? At what temperatures do plants grow best?

Think about the place you live. Is there enough warmth for plants to grow?

This is a rainforest. Many plants find it easy to grow here. It is warm but not too hot and there is plenty of water.

When is the warmest time of year? When is the coldest? Can plants grow all year?

At over 56°C, Death Valley in America is one of the hottest places on Earth.

At −89°C, Antarctica is the coldest place on Earth.

## Questions

1 Where do plants grow best? Cold places, hot places or warm places?

2 What happens when a plant gets too hot?

3 How is plant growth affected by temperature?

**Talk about it!**
Why are there no plants in Death Valley or Antarctica?

## What you have learnt

- Plants grow more slowly when it is cold.
- Plants grow more quickly when it is warm.
- Plants die when they get too cold or too hot.

**1** Here is a flowering plant.

Copy and complete these sentences.

**A** is the _____ .
**B** is the _____ .
**C** is a _____ .
**D** is the _____ .

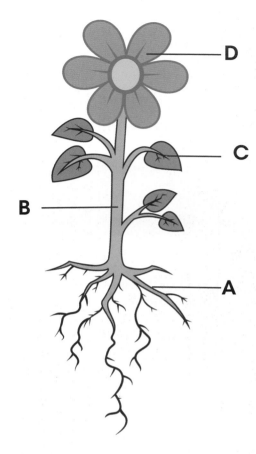

**2** Copy and complete the sentences using the missing words.

You may use each word more than once.

| roots | flowers | stem | leaves | water |
|---|---|---|---|---|

Plants have _____ that are under the ground. These hold the plant up and also absorb _____ . The water is transported to the _____ and then to the _____ and the _____ .

The _____ make food for the plant. The _____ help the plant to make seeds.

**3** Which **two** of these does a plant need for it to to grow?

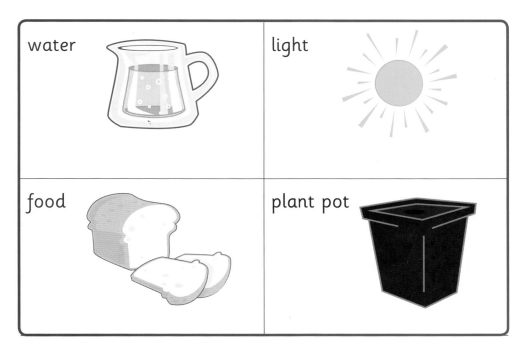

| water | light |
|-------|-------|
| food | plant pot |

Copy and complete this sentence.

A plant needs _____ and _____ to grow.

**4** Luiz and Cheng have planned an investigation.

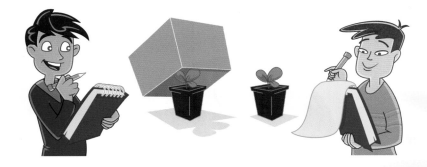

**a** What are they investigating?

**b** What do they need to keep the same to make the test fair?

**c** Which plant will grow the best?

# 2 Looking after ourselves

## 2.1 Food groups

Foods can be put into groups.

You need **dairy** foods for strong bones and teeth.

You need **fruit** and **vegetables** to be healthy.

You should not eat too much **fat** and sugar.

Food groups

You need **protein** (such as **meat** and **fish**) for growth.

You need **carbohydrate** for **energy**.

# Activity 2.1

**You will need:**
real or model food • food packaging or pictures of food • food group name cards

## Sorting food into food groups

Look at some foods and put them into food groups.
Use this book to help you.
The labels on the packets will help.

Bimla wants to be healthy. What should she eat?

Eat chocolate. Sugar gives you energy.

Eat food that tastes good.

Drink milk. It makes you strong.

Fruit and vegetables are good for you.

## Questions

1. Which food group should you eat least? Why?
2. Which food group helps you to grow?
3. What type of food group would be good to eat as a healthy snack?

**Talk about it!**
Which food groups should you eat most?

## What you have learnt

- Food can be put into groups: carbohydrate, fruit and vegetables, protein, dairy, fat.

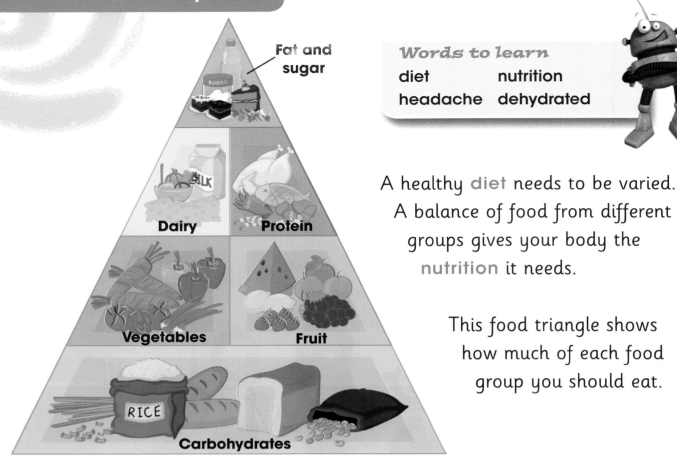

**Words to learn**

diet      nutrition
headache      dehydrated

A healthy **diet** needs to be varied. A balance of food from different groups gives your body the **nutrition** it needs.

This food triangle shows how much of each food group you should eat.

Fruit and vegetables keep us healthy. Sam will only eat bananas and carrots. He does not like any others.

## Activity 2.2

**You will need:**
some fruit and vegetables you can taste
disposable spoons

### Tasting fruit and vegetables

Talk about the taste of some fruit and vegetables.

Which ones will you like? Make a prediction then taste them.

Draw a table like this for your results.

| Fruit/Vegetable | Prediction | Result | |
| --- | --- | --- | --- |
| | Will you like it? | How did it taste? | Did you like it? |
| melon | no | very sweet | yes |
| | | | |

When running long distances it is easy to become dehydrated.

Water is part of a healthy diet. Not drinking enough will make you tired and give you a headache. This is called being dehydrated.

We can only live without water for a few days.

## Questions

1 Why do we need to eat lots of fruit and vegetables?

2 What makes people dehydrated?

**Talk about it!**
Why was it good that Sam tasted the kiwi fruit?

## What you have learnt

- A healthy diet gives your body the nutrition it needs.
- A food triangle shows how much of each food group you should eat.
- Fruit and vegetables are a very important part of a healthy diet.
- We can only live without water for a few days.

# 2.3 An unhealthy diet

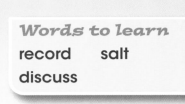

## Activity 2.3a

**You will need:**
some drinks and their labels

### Which drinks have the most sugar?

Predict which drinks are healthy and which are unhealthy. Read the labels to find out how much sugar is in each drink. Record your results in a table.

## Activity 2.3b

### What does sugar do to teeth?

**You will need:**
a drink with lots of sugar • water
egg shells • 2 plastic cups

The material that makes up egg shells is similar to the material that makes up your teeth. Look at the pictures to see what to do. Predict what you think will happen to the egg shells.

**1** Place half an egg shell into each cup.

**2** Add water to one cup and a sugary drink to the other.

**3** After seven days see what has happened to the egg shell.

Think about what you found out. Explain what too much sugar can do to your teeth.

Eating lots of fat, sugar and salt makes your diet unhealthy. Fat and salt are bad for your heart.

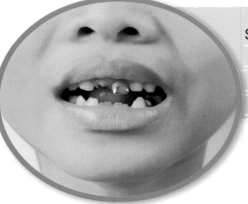

Sugar is bad for your teeth. Brushing your teeth after breakfast and before going to bed will help.

Eating too much food is bad for you. Your body can store food as fat. This can make you overweight.

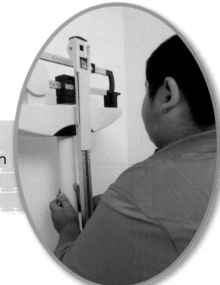

Some people do not have enough food to eat. Being very thin is not healthy.

**Challenge** Is fruit juice good for your teeth? How could you find out? **Discuss** this with your friends.

## Questions

Copy and complete these sentences.

1  Too much sugar is bad for your _____ .
2  Too much fat and salt is bad for your
    _____ .

**Talk about it!**
Why do we like to eat unhealthy food?

## What you have learnt

- Too much fat, salt and sugar in your diet will make you unhealthy.

## 2.4 Exercise and sleep

To be healthy you need to look after your body in different ways.

You need a healthy diet, exercise and sleep.

Who is doing exercise in this picture?

**Word to learn**
exercise

Exercise is lots of movement.

Playing, running and walking are all good exercise.

Exercise makes your heart, bones and muscles strong.

Sleep is also important for keeping healthy.

Most school children need 10–12 hours of sleep.

# Activity 2.4

## What happens when we exercise?

Look at the pictures to see what to do.

Heart. How fast?

Breathing. How fast?

Breathing. How fast?

Heart. How fast?

Skin. Cool or warm?

Skin. Cool or warm?

**1** at rest

**2** do some exercise

**3** after exercise

⭐ **Challenge** Predict what will happen if you exercise for longer.

## Questions

1. Which of these is exercise: running, jumping, reading, sleeping, skipping, playing football?

2. Copy and complete the sentence. Exercise is good for your _____ ,

_____

and _____ .

Even astronauts have to exercise to keep healthy.

## What you have learnt

🌀 Exercise and sleep will help to keep you healthy.

**Talk about it!**
What is a good time to go to bed?

**1** Match the food group with the description.

| 1 | dairy |
|---|---|
| 2 | carbohydrate |
| 3 | fruit and vegetables |
| 4 | fat and sugar |
| 5 | protein |

| A | do not eat too much of this |
|---|---|
| B | gives you energy |
| C | helps you to grow |
| D | keeps your body healthy |
| E | keeps your bones and teeth strong |

**2** Here is a healthy meal. Explain why it is healthy.

**3** Which sandwich is more healthy? Why?

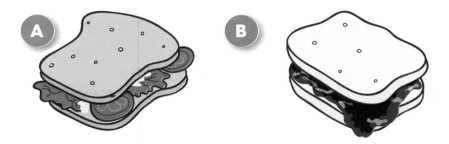

**4** These drinks have different amounts of sugar per 100ml.

Draw a table like this to show how much sugar is in each drink.

| Drink | Sugar per 100ml in g |
|-------|----------------------|
|       |                      |

Draw a bar chart to present your results.

## 3.1 Living and non-living

The plant pot is alive because it has a plant in it.

The bee is alive because it's flying.

The bee and plant are alive because they both need air.

The plant is alive because it's green.

Do you agree with what the learners say?

Which things are alive?
Which things in these pictures are alive?

Things that are alive:

- need air to breathe
- need water and food
- can move
- have senses
- can produce young
- grow
- produce waste products (excrete).

These are the seven life processes.

## Questions

1 List the **seven** life processes.

2 A horse can run, eat, drink and see. Is it alive?

3 A toy kite moves and flies in the air. Is it alive?

## Activity 3.1

### Living or non-living?

With a partner, sort pictures of things into two groups:

- living things
- non-living things.

Use the seven life processes to help you decide where to put each picture.

Were there any that you found difficult to place? If so, explain why.

**You will need:**
a large sheet of paper • pens
a selection of pictures of things that are living and non-living

## What you have learnt

All living things need air to breathe, need water and food, can move, have senses, can produce young, grow and produce waste products.

**Talk about it!**
How do you know if something is living?

# 3.2 Growth and nutrition

## Growth

Look at these pictures. Where are you now in the cycle?

baby

toddler

child

teenager

adult

All living things have young. The young grow. An **adult** is fully grown.

Name the young for each of these animals.

bear

cat

frog

Plants grow in stages.

**1** A seed.

**2** The seed begins to grow.

**3** A young plant develops.

**4** The young plant becomes a fully grown flowering plant.

## Nutrition

Animal food comes from plants and other animals. Some animals **feed** their young.

Plants make their own food. Plants use the light from the Sun and carbon dioxide from the air to make sugars. They make sugar in the green parts of the plant and release oxygen as a waste product.

## Activity 3.2

### Make a bird feeder

**You will need:**
a plastic container • string • a hole punch • fat • bird seed

Punch two holes near the top of the plastic container.
Melt the fat (get an adult to help you).
When the fat has cooled a little, stir bird seed into it.
Carefully pour the mixture into the plastic container
(do not fill it to the top).
When the mixture is cold, thread the string through the holes and hang your
bird feeder somewhere outside.

## Questions

1 What are the stages of growth for a human being?

2 How do plants make their food?

3 Where does human food
   come from?

**Talk about it!**
What food is eaten by animals that you know?

## What you have learnt

🌀 Animals and plants grow.

🌀 Plants make food by using sunlight to
   make sugars.

🌀 Animals' food comes from plants and other animals.

# 3.3 Movement and reproduction

## Movement

All animals and plants move.

Plants move slightly towards the light.

They can also spread across areas as their roots systems grow.

Their seeds can also move.

## Activity 3.3

Make a model of the moving parts of your body

**You will need:**
a template of parts of the body • split pins

Cut out the parts of the body from the template.

Use split pins to join the parts together.

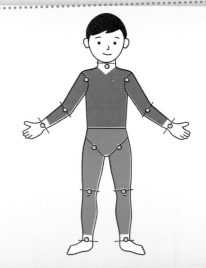

## Reproduction

Living things **reproduce** so that new animals and plants can grow to become adults. Plants make seeds. Animals and birds lay eggs or have babies.

A bird brings material to make a nest.

When animals reproduce they often make a special home for the young or the eggs. Some animals carry their young.

Two polar bear cubs with their mother at their den.

Some animals do not prepare a home. The **offspring** have to look after themselves.

Fish swim off into the sea without parents.

Caterpillars are left to look after themselves.

A baby kangaroo in its mother's pouch.

## Questions

1   Name an animal and the shelter it makes for its eggs or young.
2   Why are young caterpillars left to look after themselves?

### What you have learnt

- All animals and plants move and all living things reproduce.

**Talk about it!**

Why do some parents make a safe place for their eggs or young?

## 3.4 Sorting humans

Look at other people. They are all **similar** to you but also **different**. Our eyes are different colours.

These children all have similar bodies but there are differences. What two things are similar? What two things are different?

loop

arch

whorl

People have different shapes on their **fingerprint**.

Look at your fingers. Use a magnifying glass if possible. **Identify** which type of fingerprint you have.

## Activity 3.4

### Collecting data

Collect **data** about your classmates.
Make a chart like this to help you.

| Name | Hair colour | Eye colour | Height in m |
|------|-------------|------------|-------------|
| Sunita | black | brown | 1.21 |

Collect the names of your classmates and data about their hair, eyes and height.
Then **tally** the data on a tally chart like this one.

| Hair colour | Brown | Black | Blonde |
|-------------|-------|-------|--------|
| tally | ⊬⊦⊦ ‖ | ‖ | ‖‖ |
| total | 7 | 2 | 3 |

## Questions

1  What are the common eye colours in human beings?

2  In what ways are we the same as other people?

3  How are we different from one another?

**Talk about it!**
What differences are we born with?

## What you have learnt

🌀 People are similar in some ways but different in others.

🌀 Fingerprints are all different.

🌀 People have different hair colour, eye colour and heights.

# 3.5 Sorting living things

Scientists who study living things need to be able to **group** them.

Help the zookeeper sort the animals into the correct group.

Animals with feathers

Animals with fur

Animals with scales

Look at these pictures.
Talk to a friend about how you could sort these living things.

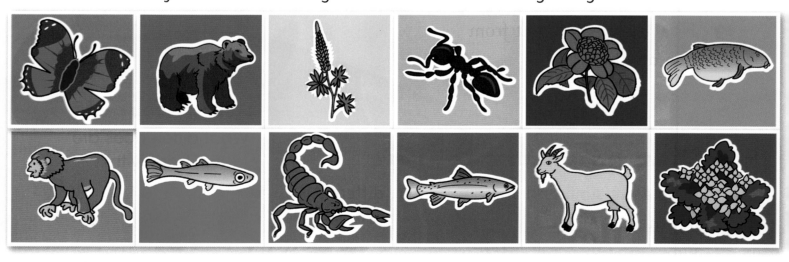

Describe the things that are similar about the things in your groups.

Juma has collected these small animals. Suggest groups he can put them in.

Suggest a question that he could use to sort the animals.

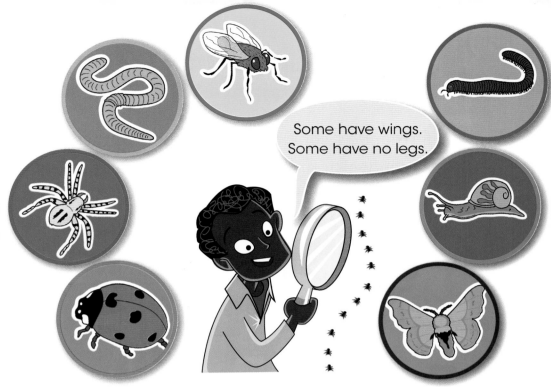

Some have wings. Some have no legs.

## Activity 3.5

### Sorting leaves

Sort your leaves into groups.
Put each group into a hoop.
Label each group.
Could you have sorted the leaves in a different way?

**You will need:**
a selection of different leaves • hoops
labels for groups

## Questions

1  How many groups of animals and plants do you know? What are they?

2  Why do scientists need to group animals?

3  Why might you group a lion and a wolf together?

**Talk about it!**
What groups do animals and plants around your home belong to?

## What you have learnt

🌀 Living things can be put into groups.
🌀 The groups have something in common.

# 3 Check your progress

**1** Magda's book contains pictures of these things. Help her to say which are alive and which are not alive.

**2** Here are some life stages of living things.

a _____ ⟶ tadpole ⟶ frog

b egg ⟶ _____ ⟶ hen

c _____ ⟶ child ⟶ adult

d seed ⟶ seedling ⟶ _____

e baby ⟶ foal ⟶ _____

Copy and complete each line. Use these words to help you.

> horse    frog spawn    chick    plant    baby

**3** Why do you think the snail is moving?

I think the snail is moving towards the light.

I think the snail is looking for a friend.

The snail looks hungry.

**4**  Salif has found this table about the number of young produced by some animals.

| Animal | Number of young produced |
|---|---|
| rabbit | 8 |
| birds | 6 |
| human | 1 or 2 |
| fish | 1000s of eggs |
| spiders | 100s of eggs |

a  Which animals can have the most young?

b  Why do some animals have many young?

**5**  Here is a plant.

For this plant, which questions are 'true' and which questions are 'false'?

a  Does the plant have green leaves?

b  Does the plant have a flower?

c  Is the plant a tree?

d  Does it have berries?

# 4 Our five senses

## 4.1 Hearing and touch

A sense is a way of finding out about the world around you.
The senses are touch, sight, hearing, smell and taste.

### Hearing

Your ears are hearing all the time.

Which of these makes the loudest sound? Which is the quietest?

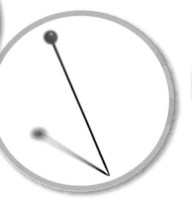

## Activity 4.1a

### Pointing at sounds

Blindfold a friend.
Make a sound.
Ask your friend to point to the source of the sound.
What can you conclude from their action?

> **You will need:**
> material to act as a blindfold • something to make a sound (small bell or two spoons)

## Touch

We have all hurt ourselves.
All of your skin can feel things touching it: hot and cold, rough and smooth, dry and wet.

## Activity 4.1b

### Touch test

Blindfold a partner.
Give your partner each item in turn (the order does not matter).
Ask them to touch each item and describe how it feels.
Can they tell you what it is?

**You will need:**
wet and dry tissues • ice cubes • sandpaper wood • plastic • metal • a blindfold

It's rough, it's very rough, it's sandpaper!

## Questions

1 How many senses do you have?
2 **a** Give an example of a very quiet sound.
  **b** Give an example of a very loud sound.
3 Where on your body is your sense of touch?

**Talk about it!**
If you were blind, how important would your other senses be?

## What you have learnt

◉ Humans have five senses: hearing, touch, taste, smell and sight.
◉ The senses work together to help humans find out about the world around them.
◉ You use your ears to hear and your skin to touch.

## 4.2 Taste and smell

A tongue has taste buds which sense tastes like salt and sweet, bitter and sour.

Taste works with smell to stop us from eating food that would make us ill.

If something smells bad it generally tastes bad too.

If your nose is blocked you cannot taste very well.

Some animals have small noses. Others have big noses.

**Words to learn**

tongue    sweet
bitter    sour

Which of these animals do you think can smell things the best?

Bears have a very good sense of smell. Bears can smell food far away.

Snakes smell with their tongues.

Animals which find their food on the ground have a good sense of smell.

## Activity 4.2

Do you like or dislike this food?

Blindfold a friend.

Ask them to taste each sample of food and say whether they like it or not.

Repeat the test but, this time, ask your friend to hold their nose so that they cannot smell the food. Does this affect how they taste the food?

**You will need:**
clean food samples on separate plates
clean spoons • plates • blindfold

## Questions

1 What part of our body do we use to taste things?

2 What part of our body do we use to smell things?

3 Why do we need to smell and taste foods?

**Talk about it!**
Why do some animals have a very good sense of smell?

## What you have learnt

⟳ The senses of taste and smell often work together.

What colour eyes do you and your friends have?

**Word to learn**
eyesight

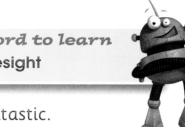

Your eyes are fantastic. They can see things close to you and much further away.

Some animals have very good **eyesight** and some animals do not.

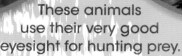
These animals use their very good eyesight for hunting prey.

This mole does not have very good eyesight. Instead, the mole uses his nose to find his way around.

Centaurus A, a galaxy that can be seen with naked eyes. It is around 12 million light years from Earth.

With our eyes we can see what is happening in the world. You can test your eyes.

## Activity 4.3

### Make and use an eye test

Choose a set of letters or numbers.
Print these in different sizes on your
piece of paper.

Fix the paper 2 or 3 metres away.

Cover one eye while you read the letters or numbers out to
check that you can see them clearly.

Now check your other eye.

Try your test with other people.

How far down the chart could you read
the letters?

Was the result the same for both eyes?
Did other people have the same result?

**You will need:**
a large piece of paper • a metre ruler
something to cover one eye

A, E, Q, R, ...

A
EQRT
JUWSP
NVOZY
BCFIDH
GKLMUX

3m

## Questions

1  Why do some animals have good eyesight?

2  Give an example of where a human needs to
   see things:
   a close up
   b at some distance away.

## What you have learnt

- Some animals have very good eyesight.
- Human eyes are a variety of colours.
- The human eye can see things that are very
  close and things that are some distance away.

**Talk about it!**
How do animals who do
not have good eyesight
find out about
their world?

# 4 Check your progress

**1** These animals have a good sense of smell.

Give two reasons why they need a good sense of smell.

**2** Alex has recorded the eye colour of the children in his school on this graph.

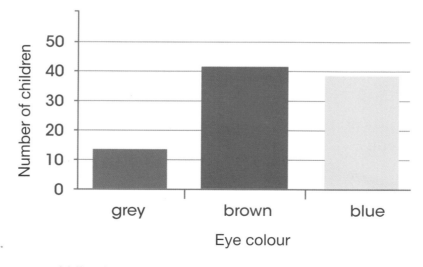

**a** Which is the most common eye colour?

**b** Which is the least common eye colour?

**3** Amal tested his friends to see which things they like and dislike.

| Name | Food | Like | Dislike |
|------|------|------|---------|
| Bill | apple | ✔ | |
|      | biscuit | ✔ | |
| Jaffa | apple | ✔ | |
|       | biscuit | ✔ | |
| Pat | apple | | ✔ |
|     | biscuit | ✔ | |
| Rava | apple | ✔ | |
|      | biscuit | ✔ | |

**a** Which food is most popular?

**b** Why do children like apples and biscuits?

**4** **a** Describe how to carry out a taste test. Include details of the equipment you would use.

**b** How could you investigate whether the sense of taste and the sense of smell are linked?

# 5 Investigating materials

## 5.1 Properties of materials

A **property** describes what a material is like.

Metal is strong but paper is weak.

Rubber is **flexible** (it can be bent) but stone is **rigid** (it keeps its shape).

Plastic is **waterproof** (water cannot get through it) but cotton is **absorbent** (it soaks up liquid).

## Activity 5.1

### A materials hunt

Find some materials.

Look carefully and feel the materials.

What properties do they have?

Draw a table like this and write down the properties of the materials.

| Material | Properties |
|----------|------------|
| paper | weak, flexible, smooth, absorbent |
| | |

Describe the properties of a material to a partner.

Can they guess which material it is?

## Questions

1 List as many different materials as you can.

2 Which material is:

   **a** silver, shiny and strong

   **b** transparent, smooth, rigid and weak?

Yuri Gagarin wore the first space suit in space in 1961.

## What you have learnt

☉ There are many different materials.

☉ Materials have many different properties.

**Talk about it!**

Which materials would you use to make a space suit?

## 5.2 Sorting materials

A material can be put in a group. These materials are sorted into hard and soft groups.

**Words to learn**

hard    soft

dull    shiny

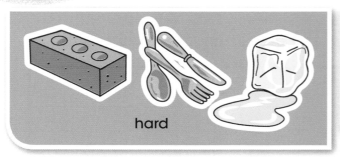

hard

soft

The same objects can also be sorted into dull and shiny groups.

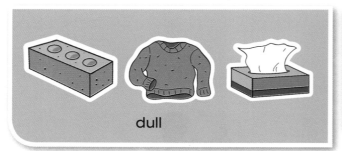

dull

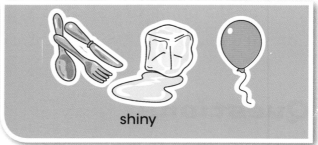

shiny

## Activity 5.2

### Sorting materials

**You will need:**

some objects each made from a single material

Look at the picture to see what to do.

Let's separate the materials as hard or soft.

Hmm, is the ball of wool hard or soft?

It's soft, so let's put it in that group.

Hard

Soft

Now choose another property and sort the objects into two different groups.

There are different ways of sorting. A branching tree database can be used to identify these four objects.

Choose one of the four objects and answer the questions.

brick

balloon

paper

ice

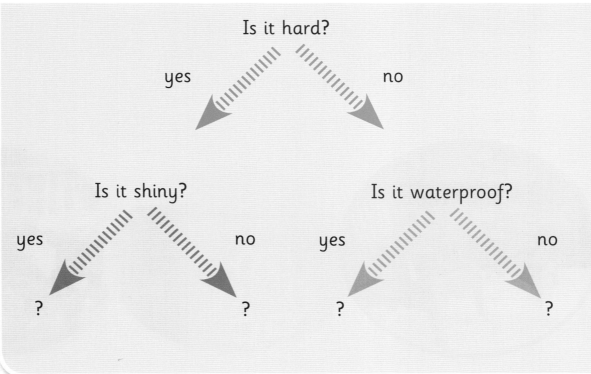

Is it hard?

yes          no

Is it shiny?          Is it waterproof?

yes          no          yes          no

?          ?          ?          ?

## Questions

1 Write **three** different materials that are waterproof.

2 Write all the properties you can think of for plastic.

Graphene is a new material that is very strong and very light.

**Talk about it!**

What could graphene be used for?

## What you have learnt

- Materials can be sorted in different ways.
- A branching tree database can be used to identify objects.

# 5.3 Uses of materials

Every material has properties. The properties make a material good for making some objects but not for others.

Here are some common materials, what they are used for, and the properties they have.

Wood is hard, strong and easy to make into objects such as chairs or bookcases.

Plastic is strong, waterproof, and easy to shape into objects such as bottles and bins.

Metal is strong, does not burn and can be sharp. Scissors, pans, knives, forks and spoons are all made from metal.

## Sensible and silly materials

Metal is a sensible material for a pan because of its properties. What would happen if the pan was made of wood?

Here are some other objects made from silly materials.

rubber bike

chocolate table

## Activity 5.3

### Why is that material useful?

Find objects in the classroom that are made of only one material.

Talk about why each object is made of that material.

On a large sheet of paper, draw a table like this. Write each observation you make in the table.

| Object | Material | Useful properties of that material |
|---|---|---|
| chair | plastic | Strong so it does not break. Flexible to make it comfy. Light so it is easy to move. |

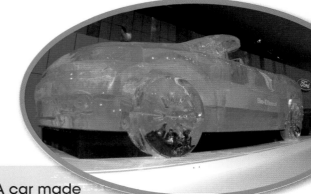

A car made from ice!

## Questions

1  Which material would be good for making sunglasses? Why?

2  A long time ago, knights used to wear metal armour. Why is metal not used for clothes?

**Talk about it!**

Why is a car made of ice a silly idea?

## What you have learnt

- How material is used depends on its properties.

# 5.4 Testing materials

## Activity 5.4a

**You will need:**
some fabrics • paper • metal foil • a small funnel
measuring cylinder • a timer

## Which material is best for an umbrella?

An umbrella needs to be waterproof.

Predict which material will be the most waterproof. The waterproof materials will not let the water through.

Look at the pictures to see what to do.

Write your results in a table.

What will you keep the same to make this test fair?

Look closely at the materials that are not waterproof. Can you see why they are not waterproof?

**1** materials to test, small funnel, measuring cylinder

Set up your equipment as shown.

**2** Place your material in the funnel.

**3** Pour water into the material and start timing.

**4** Is there any water going into the measuring cylinder?

## Activity 5.4b

### Which paper would make the strongest paper bag?

Look at the pictures to see what to do.
Predict which paper will be strongest.
How will you make this a fair test?

paper being tested

masses to add to the bag

Write your results in a table.
Look closely at the strongest paper. Can you see why it is strong?

## Questions

1  Why do the pieces of paper have to be the same size?

2  Is paper a good material for a bag? Why?

## What you have learnt

๑ Objects that need to be waterproof have to be made from waterproof materials.

๑ Objects that need to be strong have to be made of strong materials.

**Talk about it!**
How could you investigate which paper towel is the most absorbent?

Anita has a magnet. There are lots of different types of magnets.

Magnets are attracted to some materials. We say these materials are magnetic. Materials that are not attracted to magnets are non-magnetic.

Magnets can be used to separate magnetic materials from non-magnetic materials. This magnet is separating magnetic metal from other rubbish for recycling.

Sunil is trying to put a fridge magnet on the cupboard door but it keeps falling off. Why?

## Questions

1 Name a magnetic material.

2 List three materials that are not magnetic.

2 Why did Sunil's magnet not stay on the door?

## Activity 5.5

### Which materials are magnetic?

Help Sunil by testing some materials.
Look at the pictures to see what to do.

Predict which materials will be magnetic and then investigate.
Draw a table like this one for your results.

| Object | Material | Magnetic | Non-magnetic |
|--------|----------|----------|--------------|
| chair | plastic | | ✓ |

Look at your results. Can you see a pattern?
Are some materials always non-magnetic?
Which materials are magnetic?

### What you have learnt

- Some materials are magnetic.
- Many materials are non-magnetic.

**Talk about it!**

What else could we use magnets for?

**1** Write three properties for each of these materials.

The first one has been done for you.

plastic  metal  glass  paper  stone

Plastic is smooth, flexible and light.

**2** Copy this Venn diagram and write the following objects in the right places.

cotton T-shirt  wooden pencil  stone  metal paperclip  plastic ruler

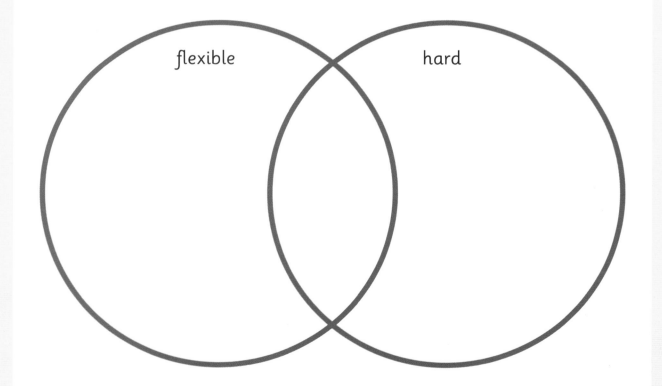

flexible        hard

**3** Draw a picture to show what will happen to the metal toy car.

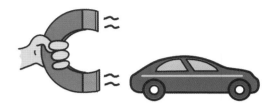

**4** Copy and complete this table.

| Object | Magnetic | Non-magnetic |
|---|---|---|
| a metal can | | |
| a book | | |
| a football | | |
| metal scissors | | |

# 6 Forces and movement

## 6.1 Push and pull

Every day you **push** and **pull** many things.
Push and pull are examples of a **force**.

Six children divide into two teams to have a tug of war.
How are the children using pushing forces and pulling
forces? What could they do so that they don't get hurt?

Each team pulls hard. They pull
with their hands.

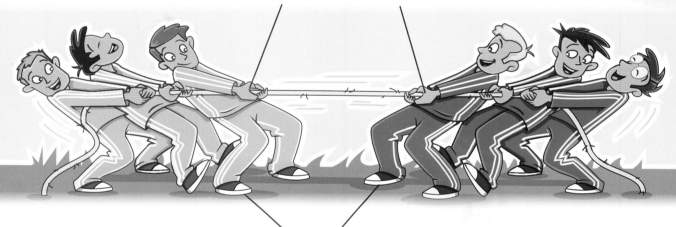

Each team pushes with their feet.

Forces can **start** and stop things moving.
They can also make things **get faster**,
**slow down** or change **direction**.

A 'great tug of war' that
involves thousands of
people is held in Naha,
Okinawa, Japan. It uses two
ropes made of rice straw.
Each rope is 2 m in diameter
and over 300 m long.

## Activity 6.1

**You will need:**
a ball • some water in a bowl
a balloon • a chair • a pencil

### Forces start and stop things moving

Work with a partner and find ways to start each of your objects moving.

See if you can feel the push or pull you are using.

Now find ways to stop each of the objects from moving.

See if you can feel the force you are using this time.

Finally, find ways to change the direction in which each object moves.

## Challenge

How could you investigate how the size of the push or pull you give to a ball affects how far it moves?

## Questions

1   Make a list of forces you have used so far today.

2   List **five** things you move with a pulling force.

3   Name a game in which you change the direction of a ball.

Magnets can be used to pick up magnetic objects.

## What you have learnt

🌀 Push and pull are examples of a force.

🌀 We can use forces to start things moving, stop things moving and change their direction.

**Talk about it!**
What have magnets got to do with forces?

## 6.2 Changing shape

Forces can change the shape of things.

This potter is using a force to create a clay pot.

A baker uses a force when making bread.

This carpenter is using a force to carve the wood.

## Activity 6.2a

### Investigating forces

**You will need:**
a ball of clay • ruler

Drop a ball of clay from a height of 5 cm.
Observe what happens to the ball of clay.
Write down your observations or draw what the clay looks like.
Shape the clay into a ball again. Drop the ball from a height of 10 cm. What is the effect on the ball of clay?
Drop the ball of clay from three more different heights.
Use ideas about forces to explain the pattern.

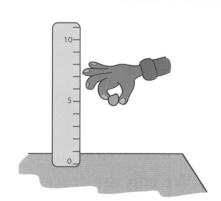

## Activity 6.2b

**You will need:**
a small, heavy ball • different objects
a paper tube

### Dropping a ball onto objects

Try using your hands to change the shape
of the objects in front of you. Which were easy to change?
Use a wide, tall paper tube to drop a heavy ball onto
the objects.
First, predict what will happen to each material. Use a table
like this.

| Object | Prediction | Result |
|---|---|---|
| biscuit | break | broke into 5 pieces |
| clay | | |
| raw vegetable | | |
| cooked vegetable | | |
| stone | | |

Plan and carry out this test. How will you make it a fair test?
Record the results.

## Questions

1. Do all materials change shape when they are pulled or
   pushed by hand?
2. List some workers who have to change
   the shape of materials.

### Talk about it!

How do forces in nature
change the shape of
the land?

## What you have learnt

🌀 Forces can change the shape of things.

## 6.3 How big is that force?

There are small forces and big forces.

Omar pulls his toys with elastic. He is pulling with more force on some toys. How can you tell that this is the case? What toy do you think needs the biggest force?

This girl is using a small force to pull on the empty sledge.

It takes a bigger force to pull this vehicle.

A volcano has so much force it can blast large rocks high in the air.

## Activity 6.3

**You will need:**
a balloon • objects to push against

### Investigating how much force

Push against different objects with a balloon until they move. The bigger the force you need to move the object, the more squashed the balloon will be.

Choose **five** objects to push against. Record your results. Say whether you used a very small force, a medium force or a large force.

## Questions

1 Put these in order from the biggest force to the smallest force:

- a horse pulling a cart
- a girl lifting a book
- a train pulling wagons
- a bird picking up a leaf.

2 Saida stretches an elastic band. Is this a pulling force or a pushing force?

All sorts of large things can be moved with a large force.

### What you have learnt

🌀 There are different sizes of force.

**Talk about it!**

How could you measure the size of a force?

# 6.4 Forcemeters

If you push on a door with foam you can see the size of the push.

**Words to learn**
forcemeter    newton

Aleksy and Peng both push on a piece of foam. We can see how hard they push.

A **forcemeter** is a piece of equipment that measures the size of a force. Forcemeters measure the size of pulls.

The unit of force is the **newton** (N). The unit is named after the famous scientist Isaac Newton, who did a lot of work on forces.

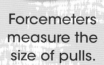

Forcemeters measure the size of pulls.

Sir Isaac Newton

## Activity 6.4

**You will need:**
a forcemeter

### Measuring forces

Use a forcemeter to measure different pulling forces around your school. Before you measure, predict which object will need the biggest force to pull it. Record the sizes of the forces in a table. Draw a bar chart to show the results. Compare your predictions with what you found out.

Tennis players use forces of different sizes to control the ball.

The forces in the ropes will be different for different climbers.

A cycle helmet must be strong enough to protect the cyclist if their head gets hurt by a force.

The wind creates a force on the sail which moves the boat through the water.

## Questions

1  What is the unit of measurement of force:

   a a newton   b a forcemeter   c a pull?

2  Why is it important for equipment for sport to be strong?

## What you have learnt

🌀 There is simple equipment which we can use to measure forces.

🌀 The unit of measurement of force is the newton.

**Talk about it!**

What could you use to measure pushing forces?

## 6.5 Friction

**Friction** is a force that acts when two surfaces rub together. Some materials cause more friction than others.

Rub your hands together. Feel them rubbing and getting warm.

When hands are rubbed together friction acts between them.

You can go very fast down a slide. There will be friction between your clothes and the surface of the slide.

Friction can start and stop things moving. You need the friction between the floor and your shoes to help you start walking.

There is friction between the bottom of your shoes and the floor which helps your shoes to **grip** the floor surface. This stops you from sliding.

Ice is slippery. There is little friction between the puck and the ice and so the puck slides easily when it is hit by the player's stick.

If you roll something across a surface, friction will cause it to slow down. It will stop at some point. Friction also help things to change direction.

The friction between the ball and the bat helps the ball to change direction.

## Activity 6.5

### Forces and friction

You can use a forcemeter to find out about friction. If there is more friction, you will need a bigger force to make something move.

Plan an investigation.

You will pull a trolley across different surfaces with a forcemeter.

Predict which surface will produce the most friction. Try using a very **smooth** surface and a **rough** surface.

How will you measure this? How will you record your results?

When you have done the test, decide what your conclusion is.

If you have time, test other surfaces.

## Questions

1 When does friction act?

2 Faye loves her garden slide. She finds that when she wears cotton clothes she goes faster than when she wears woollen clothes. Explain why.

## What you have learnt

⟳ Friction acts when two surfaces rub together.

⟳ The size of the friction force depends on the two surfaces which are rubbing together.

**Talk about it!**
Why are some shoes safer to wear on ice than others?

**1** Here is a ball bouncing toward Kamili.

- **a** How can she stop it?
- **b** How can she change the ball's direction?

**2** Which forcemeter is measuring the greatest force?

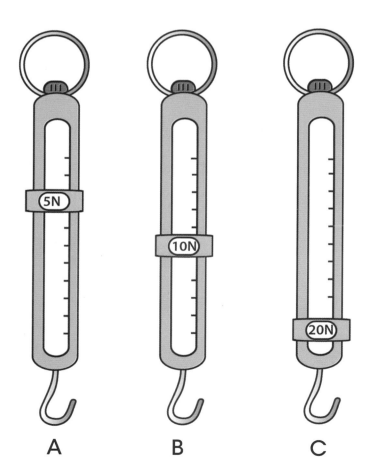

A      B      C

**3** Alex tested the force needed to pull his skateboard over different surfaces. Here are the results.

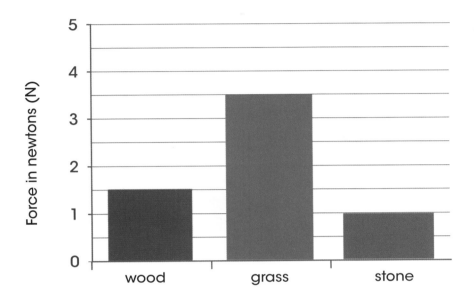

**a** Which surface was the hardest to pull the skateboard on?

**b** Which surface was the easiest to pull the skateboard on?

**4** Which surface creates the most friction with a skateboard:

- wood
- grass
- stone?

Explain your answer.

# Reference

This section of the Learner's Book covers some of the new scientific enquiry skills for this stage. They build on the skills already gained from previous stages. You should refer to these skills whenever you need them.

## How to use a ruler

Put the zero on the ruler next to the end of the object.

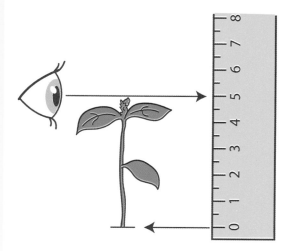 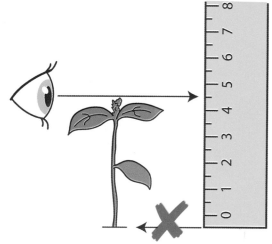

Put your eye level with the top of the object to read the scale.

Be careful. Often the zero is not at the end of the ruler.

## How to use a thermometer to measure air temperature

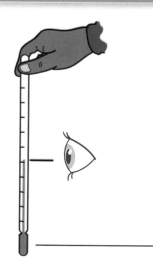

Hold the thermometer at the top.

Put your eye level with the top of the liquid to read the scale.

Do not hold the bulb or the thermometer will measure the temperature of your fingers.

## How to use a forcemeter

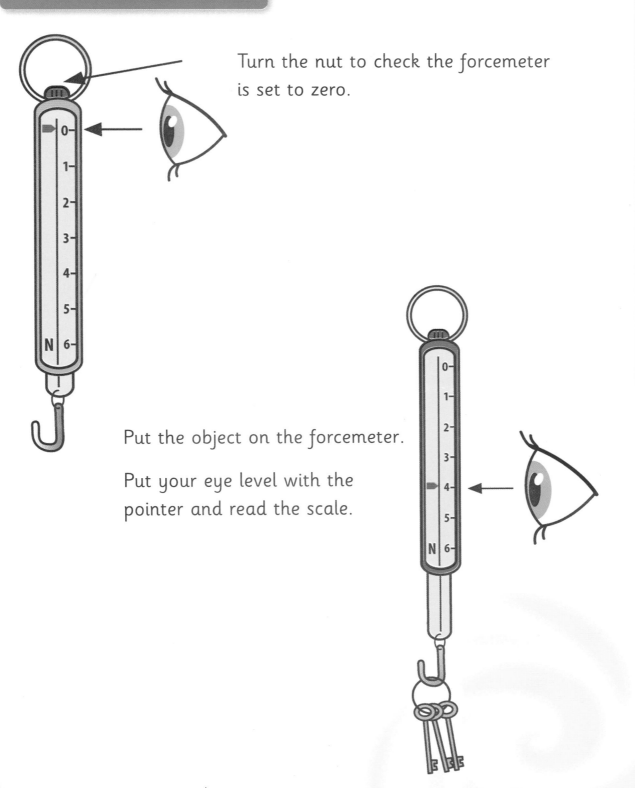

Turn the nut to check the forcemeter is set to zero.

Put the object on the forcemeter.

Put your eye level with the pointer and read the scale.

## How to present results in bar charts

| Plant height with water in cm | Plant height with no water in cm |
| --- | --- |
| 8 | 4 |

Look at the table. The numbers tell you how tall to make each bar. Draw a line at the top of the first bar. Use a ruler.

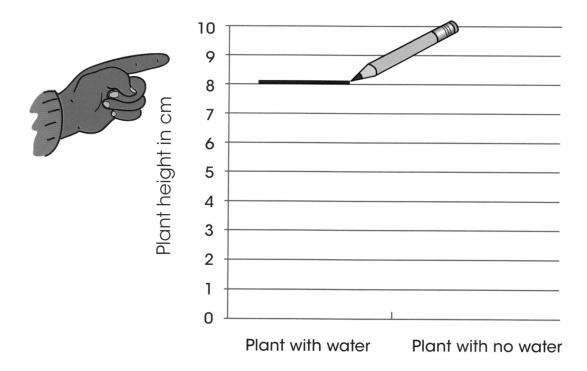

Draw the sides of the first bar. Use a ruler.

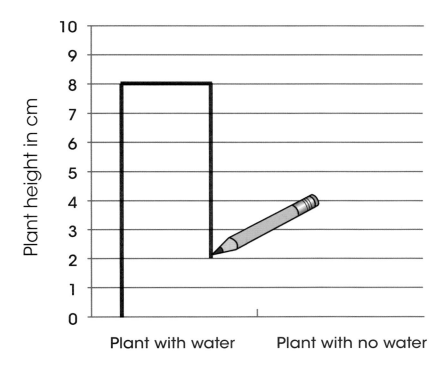

Draw the second bar the same way. Use a ruler.

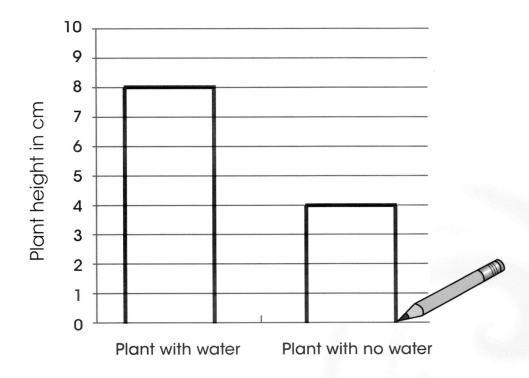

# Glossary and index

| | | |
|---|---|---|
| discuss | to talk about and share ideas | 21 |
| dull | something that is not shiny | 48 |
| effect | the result of something happening | 60 |
| energy | what is needed by humans to do any action | 16 |
| excrete | the life process of getting rid of waste | 27 |
| exercise | moving around so that your heart beats faster | 22 |
| explain | give reasons for | 9 |
| eyesight | the sense that uses your eyes to see | 42 |
| fair test | controlling a test by only changing one thing and keeping other things the same | 8 |
| fat | food that the human body stores | 16 |
| feed | bring food | 29 |
| fingerprint | the lines on the tip of a finger | 32 |
| fish | a source of protein | 16 |
| flexible | can be bent | 46 |
| flowers | part of the plant where seeds are made | 6 |

| | | |
|---|---|---|
| magnet | an object that attracts magnetic materials | 54 |
| magnetic | a material that is attracted to a magnet | 54 |
| meat | a source of protein | 16 |
| newton (N) | the unit of force – force is measured in newtons | 64 |
| non-magnetic | a material that is not attracted to a magnet | 54 |
| nutrition | the life process of getting food for health and growth | 18 |
| observe | to look closely to find things out | 60 |
| observation | things that you notice when you look closely | 51 |
| offspring | the young of an animal | 31 |
| pattern | a link between results | 55 |
| predict | to think carefully about what might happen | 8 |
| property | what something is like, for example: a mirror is smooth and shiny | 46 |
| protein | food that the human body uses for growth and repair, for example: meat and fish | 16 |
| push | to use a force to move something away from you | 58 |

| | | |
|---|---|---|
| pull | to use a force to move something towards you | 58 |
| question | a sentence that states what you would like to find out | 35 |
| record | to write or draw results to show what happened | 20 |
| reproduce | the life process of having babies, laying eggs or producing seeds | 31 |
| results | the observations or measurements made in a test | 12 |
| rigid | a rigid object keeps its shape, is not easy to bend or stretch, is not flexible | 46 |
| roots | part of plant that support the plant and collect water from the soil | 6 |
| rough | feels bumpy to touch | 67 |
| salt | small white crystals with a strong taste used in cooking | 21 |
| shiny | something that light bounces off | 48 |
| similar | when things are the same in some ways but not exactly the same | 32 |
| slow down | to move more slowly | 58 |
| smooth | something that is flat, not bumpy | 67 |

| | | |
|---|---|---|
| soft | a soft object is easy to squash, not hard | 48 |
| sort | to put things into groups | 27 |
| sour | a taste, for example: vinegar or lemon juice | 40 |
| start | to begin to do something | 58 |
| stem | part of plant that transports water around the plant | 6 |
| sweet | the taste of sugar or honey | 40 |
| tally | a way of counting by drawing lines in groups of five | 33 |
| temperature | how hot or cold something is | 12 |
| thermometer | an object used to measure temperature | 12 |
| tongue | part of the body you use to taste things | 40 |
| transport | to move something | 6 |
| unhealthy | being unfit, unwell, sick or poorly | 7 |
| vegetables | the part of a plant that is grown to be eaten | 16 |
| waterproof | something that water cannot get through | 46 |
| wilt | to lose shape, become limp | 8 |
| young | not fully grown | 27 |

# Acknowledgements

The authors and publisher are grateful for the permissions granted to reproduce copyright materials. While every effort has been made, it has not always been possible to identify the sources of all the materials used, or to trace all the copyright holders.
If any omissions are brought to our notice, we will be happy to include the appropriate acknowledgements on reprinting.
The publisher is grateful to the experienced teachers Lynne Ransford and Mansoora Shoaib Shah for their careful reviewing of the content.

p. 7*tr* somchai rakin/ Shutterstock; p. 7*bl* Nigel Cattlin/ Alamy; p. 7*tl* silver-john/ Shutterstock; p. 7*br* Margrit Hirsch/ Shutterstock; p. 9 Andrzej Wojcicki/ Science Photo Library; p. 10*l* / GAP Photos; p. 10*c* Martin Shields/ Alamy; p. 10*r* / GAP Photos; p. 13*tr* Frank Schwere/Stone/ Getty Images; p. 13*bl* Anatoliy Lukich/ Shutterstock; p. 13*br* Seth Resnick/Science Faction/ Getty Images; p. 16*cl* Food Features/ Alamy; p. 16*bc* Elena Schweitzer/ Shutterstock; p. 16*br* Valentyn Volkov/ Shutterstock; p. 16*tr* Adisa/ Shutterstock; p. 16*tl* Christian Draghici/ Shutterstock; p. 18 Matthew Cole/ Shutterstock; p. 19 arekmalang/ Shutterstock; p. 21*tl* yadom/ Shutterstock; p. 21*tr* bikeriderlondon/ Shutterstock; p. 21*bl* Peter Turnley/ Corbis; p. 23 European Space Agency/Anneke Le Floc'h/ Science Photo Library; p. 26*tl* Robnroll/ Shutterstock; p. 26*tcl* Alexander Sviridenkov/ Shutterstock; p. 26*tcr* Leonard Zhukovsky/ Shutterstock; p. 26*tr* Peter Wey/ Shutterstock; p. 26*bl* Jason and Bonnie Grower/ Shutterstock; p. 26*bcl* Vilainecrevette/ Shutterstock; p. 26*bcr* IbajaUsap/ Shutterstock; p. 26*br* Horiyan/ Shutterstock; p. 28*l* GP232/ iStockphoto; p. 28*c* Hofhauser/ Shutterstock; p. 28*r* StevenRussellSmithPhotos/ Shutterstock; p. 29 Iakov Kalinin/ Shutterstock; p. 31*l* Bruce Lichtenberger/Photolibrary/ Getty Images; p. 31*tr* Darrell Gulin/Stockbyte/ Getty Images; p. 31*br* mark higgins/ Shutterstock; p. 38*l* Realimage/ Alamy; p. 38*tr* Racefotos2008/ Shutterstock; p. 38*cl* Darrin Jenkins/ Alamy; p. 38*cr* CharlesKnox/ iStockphoto; p. 41*l* Thomas Sbampato/imagebroker/ Alamy; p. 41*r* almondd/ Shutterstock; p. 42*tl* Hilary Brodey/Photodisc/ Getty Images; p. 42*tc* Khakimullin Aleksandr/ Shutterstock; p. 42*tr* Pressmaster/ Shutterstock; p. 42*cl* neelsky/ Shutterstock; p. 42*c* PRILL/ Shutterstock; p. 42*cr* David Cole/ Alamy; p. 42*bl* Robert Gendler/Visuals Unlimited, Inc./ Getty Images; p. 47 World Perspectives/ Stone/ Getty Images; p. 49 Andre Geim, Kostya Novoselov/ Science Photo Library; p. 50*l* Andreas von Einsiedel/ Alamy; p. 50*c* IS2009-03/Image Source/ Alamy; p. 50*r* Pete Ryan/National Geographic Image Collection/ Alamy; p. 51 Matthew Richardson/ Alamy; p. 54 paul ridsdale/ Alamy; p. 58 AFP/ Getty Images; p. 59 MilanB/ Shutterstock; p. 60*l* Jetta Productions/Dana Neely/ Getty Images; p. 60*c* Xiaojiao Wang/ Shutterstock; p. 60*r* Nagy-Bagoly Arpad/ Shutterstock; p. 62*tl* Maria Uspenskaya/ Shutterstock; p. 62*tr* imac / Alamy; p. 62*br* andersenoystein/ iStockphoto; p. 63 Mark Burnett/ Alamy; p. 64*l* Andrew Lambert Photography/ Science Photo Library; p. 64*r* Sir Godfrey Kneller/The Bridgeman Art Library/ Getty Images; p. 65*l* Stuart Slavicky/ Shutterstock; p. 65*cl* i love images / active/ Alamy; p. 65*cr* Ljupco Smokovski/ Shutterstock; p. 65*r* Taiga/ Shutterstock; p. 66*tl* PT Images/ Shutterstock; p. 66*tr* drbimages/ iStockphoto; p. 66*br* Aspen Photo/ Shutterstock; p. 66*bl* Trevor Lush/UpperCut Images/ Alamy

*l* = left, *r* = right, *t* = top, *b* = bottom, *c* = centre

Cover artwork: Bill Bolton